THE
PRACTICE
OF
JOY

Reflective Flip Book

CREATING REVOLUTIONARY CHANGE IN OUR
PERSONAL AND PROFESSIONAL LIVES

Pamela Larde, PhD

I0179289

The Practice of Joy Reflective Flip Book

Tandem Light Press 2024

ISBN: 979-8-9882517-9-8

INSTRUCTIONS

HOW TO USE THESE CARDS

This self-guided or practitioner-guided flip book is organized into eight key categories that culminate into the practice of joy as a holistic approach to life. These categories include:

1. Joy Resilience
2. Practices of Joy
3. Self-Love
4. Communities of Joy
5. Mental Stamina
6. The Reverse Domino Effect
7. Ethics of Joy
8. Revolutionary Joy

Spend a minimum of one week on each category working to integrate each concept into your life. Begin daily by reading the concept out loud, followed by the reflection and affirmation on the following page. Keeping a journal to note key reflections and experiences is highly recommended. This 8-week process is best accomplished in community with others, but can also be effective as a solo project for anyone deeply committed to integrating joy into their lives.

RESOURCES & SUPPORT

RESOURCES & SUPPORT

There are several resources available that can accompany this experience, including:

Books (find at at all major booksellers & www.DrPamelaLarde.com):
- Joyfully Single: A Guide to Enlightenment, Wholeness, Change
- The Practice of Joy Workbook

Communities:
- The Joy Resilience Community: www.thejoyresiliencecommunity.mn.co
- The Joy Whisperer Podcast: www.TheJoyWhisperer.com
- Dr. Pamela Larde's website: www.DrPamelaLarde.com

Social Media Pages:
- Instagram & TikTok: @joyresearcher
- LinkedIn: Dr. Pamela Larde

Mental Health Support:
- Suicide Hotline: Text 988, Call 800-985-5990
- Better Help (downloadable therapy app): www.betterhelp.com

Dr. Pamela Larde
THE PRACTICE & SCIENCE OF JOY

JOY RESILIENCE

With the understanding that joy is a way of being and happiness is a response to positive events, joy resilience is an approach to life that taps into well-being as a source of strength through struggle.

Happiness

soothing

reactive

externally stimulated

conditional

fleeting

well-being not required

wellness-enhancing

energizing

contagious

stress relieving

Joy

internally & externally stimulated

enduring

transformative

intentional

values-driven

rooted in well-being

Dr. *Pamela Larde*
THE PRACTICE & SCIENCE OF JOY

1

JOY RESILIENCE

Reflect on Joy in Challenges

Think about a difficult time when you found a moment of joy.
How did this joy impact your ability to cope with the challenge?

Affirmation

"In every challenge I face today,
I will find joy to uplift
and strengthen me."

2

JOY RESILIENCE

Reflect on the Small Daily Joys

Reflect on the small, everyday joys that you might often overlook. How do these moments contribute to your overall resilience?

Affirmation

"Every small joy is a building block of my resilience."

3

JOY RESILIENCE

Reflect on Joy in Relationships

Consider the joy that comes from your relationships. How does this joy fortify you during tough times?

Affirmation

"The joy in my relationships
is a powerful source of strength."

4

JOY RESILIENCE

Reflect on the Joy of Learning

Reflect on a recent learning experience,
even if it was challenging. How did the joy of learning
and growing help you through it?

Affirmation

"The joy of learning and growing
makes me resilient."

5

JOY RESILIENCE

Reflect on the Joy in Self-Care

What activities that bring you joy and
contribute to your self-care?
How do they help your resilience?

Affirmation

"Self-care activities that bring me joy
are essential to my resilience."

6

JOY RESILIENCE

Reflect on Past Struggles

Look back at a past struggle and identify
moments of joy that helped you.
How can you seek similar joy in future challenges?

Affirmation

"I remember to seek joy through my struggles, as it
is my anchor and strength."

7

JOY RESILIENCE

Reflect on Gratitude for Joyful Moments

Reflect on the power of savoring micro moments of joy. How does being grateful for joyful moments increase your resilience?

Affirmation

"I am grateful for every joyous moment, as these moments reinforce my resilience."

PRACTICES OF JOY

This is the idea that we engage in at least one of four key practices to integrate joy into our lives. This includes the emotion, ethos, experience, and expression of joy.

EXPERIENCE

How I welcome or create opportunities to indulge in joy.

EMOTION

How I physiologically respond to joyful moments.

Four Practices of Joy

How my character and my values embody and reflect joy.

ETHOS

How I outwardly demonstrate that I am experiencing joy.

EXPRESSION

DR. *Pamela Larde*
THE PRACTICE & SCIENCE OF JOY

1

PRACTICES OF JOY

Reflect on Recognizing Joy

Reflect on how you recognize and feel joy
as an emotion. What are the signs that tell you
you're experiencing joy?

Affirmation

"I am in tune with my emotions
and recognize joy in its purest form."

2

PRACTICES OF JOY

Reflect on an Ethos of Living Joyfully

Consider how joy influences your character and decisions. How do you incorporate an ethos of joy in your values and beliefs?

Affirmation

"My ethos is rooted in joy, guiding me to live a life of positivity and purpose."

3

PRACTICES OF JOY

Reflect on Experiencing Joyful Moments

Reflect on a recent experience that brought you joy. How did this experience enrich your life and perspective?

Affirmation

"Every joyful experience I encounter enriches my life and broadens my perspective."

4

PRACTICES OF JOY

Reflect on Sharing Joy

Think about how you express joy and share it with others. What are your unique ways of spreading joy?

Affirmation

"I freely express and share my joy, uplifting myself and those around me."

5

PRACTICES OF JOY

Reflect on the Emotion of Joy

Reflect on how the emotion of joy helps you to be resilient in difficult times. How does joy help you bounce back?

Affirmation

"Joy fortifies my emotional resilience, helping me to overcome challenges with grace."

6

PRACTICES OF JOY

Reflect on the Ethics of Joy

Consider how a joyful ethos affects your ethical decisions. How does joy influence your sense of right and wrong?

Affirmation

"My joy shapes my ethical choices, leading me towards kindness and integrity."

7

PRACTICES OF JOY

Reflect on Learning & Teaching Joy

What have you learned about joy? How you teach or express these lessons to others? How do these experiences impact your life?

Affirmation

"I am both a student and teacher of joy, continuously learning and spreading its wisdom."

SELF-LOVE

We grow in self-love as we experience four different approaches to loving ourselves in response to our life circumstances. These elements include: survivalist, superficial, romantic, and infinite.

Elements of Self-Love

Survivalist
the natural instinct to fight for our lives

Romantic
falling in love with our transformed selves

Superficial
practicing self-love when we don't yet feel it

Infinite
a limitless and liberating form of self-love

Dr. *Pamela Larde*
THE PRACTICE & SCIENCE OF JOY

1

SELF-LOVE

Reflect on Survival

Reflect on how loving yourself has been a crucial part of your survival. How has this form of self-love shown up in your life?

Affirmation

"My love for myself is a fundamental part of my survival and strength."

2

SELF-LOVE

Reflect on Superficial Self-Love

Consider the times when your self-love was driven by aspirations rather than actual self-appreciation. How has this superficial self-love helped you grow?

Affirmation

"Even when my self-love feels superficial, it's a stepping stone towards genuine growth and appreciation."

3

SELF-LOVE

Reflect on Romantic Self-Love

Reflect on a moment of significant achievement or positive change that spiked your self-love. How did this romantic self-love enhance your self-esteem?

Affirmation

"Major accomplishments boost my self-love, affirming my worth and achievements."

4

SELF-LOVE

Reflect on Infinite Self-Love

Think about the times when you've experienced a strong, enduring love for yourself. How does this infinite self-love manifest in your daily life?

Affirmation

"I possess a deep, infinite love for myself that sustains and nurtures me in all aspects of life."

5

SELF-LOVE

Reflect on Growth Through Self-Love

Reflect on how your journey through different types of self-love has contributed to your personal growth.

Affirmation

"Each stage of self-love I experience contributes to my ongoing growth and self-discovery."

6

SELF-LOVE

Reflect on Self-Love in Challenges

Consider how your approach to self-love has helped you during challenging times. How has it been a source of resilience?

Affirmation

"My self-love is a source of resilience, guiding me through life's challenges with grace and strength."

7

SELF-LOVE

Reflect on the Evolution of Self-Love

Reflect on the evolution of your self-love journey from survivalist to infinite. How has this evolution changed your perspective on life and yourself?

Affirmation

"As my self-love evolves, so does my understanding and appreciation of myself and my journey."

COMMUNITIES OF JOY

Our communities of joy encompass the collective of people who surround us that either add to or diminish our joy. This includes our core, circle, and fragmented communities.

Communities of Joy Model

FRAGMENTED COMMUNITY

Jealousy

Fear

Maliciousness

Indifference

CIRCLE COMMUNITY

Kindness

Support

Affirmation

Intellectual
Compatibilty

CORE COMMUNITY

Belief
Commitment
Loyalty
Adoration

Dr. Pamela Larde
THE PRACTICE & SCIENCE OF JOY

1

COMMUNITIES OF JOY

Reflect on Intimacy & Trust

Reflect on your core community. How do the intimacy and trust within this group contribute to your joy?

Affirmation

"I cherish my core community, whose intimacy and trust enrich my life with profound joy."

2

COMMUNITIES OF JOY

Reflect on Social Bonds

Think about your circle connections. How do these relationships, though less intimate, add value and joy to your life?

Affirmation

"My circle connections bring diverse perspectives and joy into my life, enhancing my social experience."

3

COMMUNITIES OF JOY

Reflect on Learning & Boundaries

Reflect on your interactions with members of your fragmented communities. What have these interactions taught you about setting boundaries and finding joy?

Affirmation

"Even in fragmented communities,
I learn valuable lessons and set boundaries
that preserve my joy."

4

COMMUNITIES OF JOY

Reflect on Support & Comfort

Consider how your core community provides support and comfort in times of need. How does this impact your sense of joy?

Affirmation

"The support and comfort I receive from my core community are pillars of my joy."

5

COMMUNITIES OF JOY

Reflect on Networking & Opportunities

Reflect on how your circle community offers networking and opportunities.
How do these connections contribute to your personal and professional joy?

Affirmation

"My circle community opens doors to new opportunities, adding to my joy and growth."

6

COMMUNITIES OF JOY

Reflect on Resilience & Understanding

Think about how dealing with fragmented communities has built your resilience and understanding of different perspectives.

Affirmation

"My fragmented communities strengthen my resilience and broaden my understanding, contributing to a balanced sense of self."

7

COMMUNITIES OF JOY

Reflect on Harmony Among Communities

Reflect on how you maintain harmony between these different communities and how this balance contributes to your overall joy.

Affirmation

"I skillfully balance my core, circle, and fragmented communities to create a harmonious and joyful life."

MENTAL STAMINA

Mental stamina is a strategy for pushing forward and persisting through tough, unpredictable situations by engaging with people, projects, prayer, practice, and patience.

PEOPLE
Friends & family
Helping professionals
Support groups

PATIENCE
Affirmations about patience
Mindset shifting strategies
Personal strength building

PROJECTS
That energize
That serve others
That tap into the creative
part of the brain

STRATEGIES
for Mental
Stamina

PRACTICE
That keep the body moving
That yields positivity
That keeps us connected to
close ones

PRAYER
That encourages
That calms
That expresses gratitude

DR. *Pamela Larde*
THE PRACTICE & SCIENCE OF JOY

1

MENTAL STAMINA

Reflection on Resilience

Consider a time when you faced a challenging situation. How did engaging with people, projects, prayer, practice, or patience help you overcome it?

Affirmation

"I am stronger because of the challenges I face."

2

MENTAL STAMINA

Reflect on Adaptability

Think about how you adapt to unpredictable situations. In what ways can you can improve?

Affirmation

"I embrace uncertainty and adapt with resilience."

3

MENTAL STAMINA

Reflect on Support Systems

Reflect on the role of your support network in building your mental stamina. How crucial have they been in your journey?

Affirmation

"I am thankful for the people who support and strengthen me."

4

MENTAL STAMINA

Reflect on the Power of Practice

How do your daily practices and routines contribute to your ability to persist through tough times?

Affirmation

"My practices and routines build my mental stamina every day."

5

MENTAL STAMINA

Reflect on Patience & Progress

Consider how patience has played a role in your personal and professional growth. How can you improve?

Affirmation

"I am patient with myself
and my progress."

6

MENTAL STAMINA

Reflect on Learning from Setbacks

Think about a recent setback. What did it teach you about your persistence and mental stamina?

Affirmation

"Every setback is a step forward
in my journey of growth."

7

MENTAL STAMINA

Reflect on Gratitude for Growth

Reflect on the personal growth you've achieved through practicing mental stamina.

Affirmation

"I am capable of handling tough situations with grace and strength."

THE REVERSE DOMINO EFFECT

The reverse domino effect is the journey from trauma to personal growth involving belief, acceptance, hope, determination, and growth.

The Reverse Domino Effect

MILESTONE 1: ACCEPTANCE

Mindset:
My story strengthens me.

Strategy:
Stand in your truth.

MILESTONE 2: BELIEF

Mindset:
I trust the power of my voice.

Strategy:
Give voice to your inner voice.

MILESTONE 3: HOPE

Mindset:
What I want is possible.

Strategy:
Recreate your future.

MILESTONE 4: DETERMINATION

Mindset:
I am energized and driven.

Strategy:
Activate your dreams.

MILESTONE 5: GROWTH

Mindset:
I am transforming.

Strategy:
Introduce yourself to you.

Dr. *Pamela Larde*
THE PRACTICE & SCIENCE OF JOY

1

THE REVERSE DOMINO EFFECT

Reflect on Self-Healing

Reflect on your belief in your ability to heal and grow from trauma. How has this belief shaped your healing journey?

Affirmation

"I believe in my ability to heal and grow stronger from my experiences."

2

THE REVERSE DOMINO EFFECT

Reflect on Acceptance of the Past

Consider how accepting the whole of your experience can be a step towards healing. What can acceptance teach you?

Affirmation

"I accept my past and understand that it is a chapter in my journey, not my entire story."

3

THE REVERSE DOMINO EFFECT

Reflect on Hope for the Future

Reflect on how hope has guided you through tough times. How has maintaining hope changed your outlook on life?

Affirmation

"The hope I carry lights my path and guides me towards a brighter future."

Dr. Pamela Larde
THE PRACTICE & SCIENCE OF JOY

4

THE REVERSE DOMINO EFFECT

Reflect on Determination

Think about the times when your determination has helped you overcome challenges related. How has this determination manifested in your life?

Affirmation

"My determination is unbreakable, and it empowers me to overcome any obstacle."

5

THE REVERSE DOMINO EFFECT

Reflect on Growth in the Journey

Reflect on the growth you've experienced as a result of your journey.
How have you changed and evolved?

Affirmation

"Every step in my journey adds to my growth, making me stronger and wiser."

Dr. Pamela Larde
THE PRACTICE & SCIENCE OF JOY

6

THE REVERSE DOMINO EFFECT

Reflect on Strength in Vulnerability

How has acknowledging and embracing your vulnerabilities contributed to your personal growth? What strengths have you discovered?

Affirmation

"In my vulnerability lies my strength, paving the way for genuine growth and healing."

7

THE REVERSE DOMINO EFFECT

Reflect on Empowerment & Healing

Reflect on how the process of healing from trauma has empowered you. How has this empowerment manifested in your personal and professional life?

Affirmation

"I am empowered by my healing journey. This strength radiates in every aspect of my life."

ETHICS OF JOY

The ethics of joy describing how our state of wellness and sources of joy inform our mindset, values, and behaviors. This means deciphering between the languishing well (toxic & malicious joy) and the flourishing well (authentic & vicarious joy).

THE ETHICS OF JOY

The Languishing Well

Regressive Joy

Toxic (toward self)
Malicious (toward others)

The Flourishing Well

Progressive Joy

Authentic (toward self)
Vicarious (toward others)

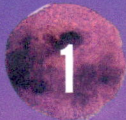

1

ETHICS OF JOY

Reflect on a Mindset Informed by Joy

Reflect on how your sources of joy shape your mindset. How consistently do you find yourself drawing from the flourishing well?

Affirmation

"I choose a mindset shaped by authentic joy to create positivity and well-being."

2

ETHICS OF JOY

Reflect on Values Guided by Joy

Consider how your joy influences your values.
Are your values aligned with the flourishing
well of vicarious and authentic joy?

Affirmation

"My values are guided by authentic and
vicarious joy, steering me towards ethical
and compassionate choices."

3

ETHICS OF JOY

Reflect on Behaviors Driven By Joy

Reflect on how your sources of joy impact your behavior. How do your behaviors and life outomes reflect the flourishing well?

Affirmation

"I choose behaviors that reflect authentic joy. This enriches my life and those around me."

4

ETHICS OF JOY

Reflect on Resisting the Languishing Well

Think about times you might have drawn joy from the languishing well. How have you redirected yourself towards healthier sources of joy?

Affirmation

"I consciously reject toxic sources of joy and embrace healthier, more fulfilling alternatives."

5

ETHICS OF JOY

Reflect on Embracing Authentic Joy

Reflect on what authentic joy means to you. How do you cultivate and maintain this form of joy in your life?

Affirmation

"I embrace and cultivate authentic joy, recognizing it as the foundation of my ethical living."

6

ETHICS OF JOY

Reflect on Learning from Vicarious Joy

Consider the role of vicarious joy in your life. How does experiencing joy through others' achievements and happiness influence your ethics and actions?

Affirmation

"Vicarious joy enhances my empathy and joyfulness, enriching my ethical understanding and connections."

7

ETHICS OF JOY

Reflecting on Balancing Joy Sources

Reflect on how you balance drawing joy from different sources. How does this balance contribute to your overall wellness and ethical choices?

Affirmation

"I maintain a healthy balance in my sources of joy, ensuring it nourishes my wellness and ethical decisions."

REVOLUTIONARY JOY

Revolutionary joy is enacted when we embrace our purpose identity and embody a worldview of joy to seek justice and liberation for ourselves and others through a process of enlightenment, wholeness, and change.

THE REVOLUTIONARY JOY MODEL

ENLIGHTENMENT
- Understanding
- Perception
- Joy Integration
- Strategy

CHANGE
- Purpose Identity
- Personal Advocacy
- Social Advocacy

WHOLENESS
- Acceptance
- Belief
- Hope
- Determination
- Growth

Dr. Pamela Larde
THE PRACTICE & SCIENCE OF JOY

1

REVOLUTIONARY JOY

Reflect on Purpose and Joy

How does your sense of purpose align with your experiences of joy? How does this alignment drive you to create change?

Affirmation

"My purpose fuels my joy, and together they guide me to enact positive change."

2

REVOLUTIONARY JOY

Reflect on Past Struggles

Reflect on a time when you used joy as a strength while advocating for justice. How did this joy impact your efforts?

Affirmation

"In my pursuit of justice,
joy is my strength and my shield."

3

REVOLUTIONARY JOY

Reflect on a Life Approach of Joy

How does a life approach centered on joy influence your approach to challenges and injustices? How does it shape your actions?

Affirmation

"With a life approach of joy, I confront challenges and injustices proactively."

4

REVOLUTIONARY JOY

Reflect on Joy in Community

Reflect on the role of joy in building and nurturing communities. How does shared joy strengthen collective efforts for change?

Affirmation

"Shared joy in my community amplifies our collective power to create change."

5

REVOLUTIONARY JOY

Reflect on Transformative Joy

Think about a situation where your joy led to transformative change. What did this teach you about the power of joy?

Affirmation

"The transformative power of my joy creates ripples of positive change."

6

REVOLUTIONARY JOY

Reflect on Joy and Resilience

Reflect on how using joy as a tool
enhances your resilience
in the face of adversity and struggle.

Affirmation

"Joy is a tool for resilience, empowering
me to overcome with determination."

7

REVOLUTIONARY JOY

Reflect on Inspirational Joy

Consider how your joy can inspire and compel others to join in the pursuit of justice and positive change.

Affirmation

"My joy inspires others, creating a united front for justice and change."